REAL ID

Seven Emotional Steps to Unlocking the Real You

Dr. Tiffany Ross

Biloxi, Mississippi

ISBN: <u>979-8-218-92756-1</u>

Library of Congress Control Number: 2026902490

Published by Dr. Tiffany Ross
United States of America

For additional resources, coaching, bookings, and community, visit: www.drtiffanyross.com

Table of Contents

DEDICATION

To my family and friends who have prayed, encouraged, and pushed me to embrace my own identity, I appreciate you. And to everyone woman that have trusted me on their own healing journeys, I salute you!

ACKNOWLEDGEMENTS

To my husband, Vaughn—
thank you for loving me through every version of
myself I was still learning to understand. Your
covering, patience, and unwavering belief in me
gave me the space to heal, grow, and fully step into
who I was always called to be.

To my children—Ky, Korey, Stephen, and
Nathaniel—
you are my "why." Everything I confronted, broke,
and rebuilt within myself was so you would never
have to carry what was never yours. May this book
remind you that wholeness is your birthright.

To my pastors, DeWayne and Valinda
Willingham—
thank you for your unwavering support,
encouragement, and spiritual covering. Your
leadership has been a constant source of strength
and guidance in my journey.

To my spiritual father, Dr. Joshua P. Smith—
thank you for being a pioneer and a bridge in my
life. Your influence helped me see what was

possible in merging faith and mental health, and gave me the courage to walk boldly in that calling.

And to every woman doing the hard, unseen work of healing—this is for you.

INTRODUCTION

If I told you how many times I've started and stopped this book, you might second-guess reading it at all. I wish I were exaggerating—but I'm not. Because I believe God has called me to live a life of transparency, I'm going to honor that calling here. This book took nearly two years to write, not because I lacked the words, but because I lacked belief in the words I already had. I did not believe they were powerful enough to make an impact. More honestly, I did not believe there was greatness inside of *me.* That belief—or lack of it—didn't come out of nowhere.

My husband and I often find ourselves in deep conversations about our pasts and how those experiences quietly shaped who we are today. During one of our late-night pillow talk sessions, I was reminded of a moment from high school that forever altered the trajectory of my life.

I became a mother at sixteen. The odds were already stacked against me. But my adopted mother—who was also my great aunt—refused to let my circumstances define my future. At the end of my tenth-grade year, she *made* me attend summer school. Not as a suggestion. As a mandate. Those courses positioned me to graduate a full year early, causing me to skip eleventh grade entirely. That single decision changed the direction of my life for decades to follow. At that time, I couldn't see the significance of it. I only knew it was uncomfortable, inconvenient, and hard. Sometimes love shows up disguised as pressure.

That same year, I had an English teacher named Mrs. Anderson—one of only a few Black teachers in our predominantly segregated community. One day, she assigned us to write a poem. When she returned my paper, she didn't just grade it. She *saw* it. She showed me how, without realizing it, I had shaped my words into the outline of an angel. I remember feeling stunned, overwhelmed, and teary-eyed. I didn't understand it then, but I believe now that God was showing me something important: *I was not alone.* Even in seasons where I couldn't recognize my own worth, He had already assigned guardians to my life.

Psalm 91:11 (**New International Version**) says,

"For He will command His angels concerning you to guard you in all your ways."

That moment planted a seed—one that would take years to fully bloom.

Why You Haven't Fully Stepped into Your Real Identity

There are three core reasons that I believe many people struggle to recognize and walk in their real identity—and they are the very reasons this book exists.

The first reason is in the area of your calling and maturity. Calling often arrives before confidence, because you haven't yet matured into it. This is why others will see it before you do. Growth has a timing, and with that timing comes healing and maturity. When you heal and mature in one area, it will prepare you for healing in other areas.

The next core reason is in your self-worth. You may repeatedly dismiss or undervalue yourself. When you normalize what is extraordinary about you, you unintentionally minimize your impact.

Lastly—and this is the most common—something traumatic may have happened to you. Trauma creates emotional blockages that drain self-confidence, distort identity, and make trust feel unsafe. Left unattended, these wounds quietly shape how you show up in relationships, leadership, and life. To fully step into the fullness of who you really are, you must be willing to declutter and mend **seven primary emotional spaces**. Healing is not passive. It is intentional. And it requires honesty. This book is your guide through those spaces—one step at a time.

The Seven Emotional Spaces

Transformational Self-Care

Transformational self-care is not about spa days, vacations, or journaling alone. It is about refusing to abandon yourself. Many ambitious women give endlessly while ignoring their internal pain. This chapter teaches you how to care for your mind, body, and soul without guilt—and without self-neglect.

Mother Wounds

Unresolved wounds from the first woman in your life can deeply impact how you relate to other women—and to yourself. This chapter helps you confront, process, and heal maternal wounds with compassion and self-acceptance, allowing you to embrace who God created you to be.

Father Wounds

Fathers impart identity and self-security. When a father is absent, inconsistent, or emotionally unavailable, daughters often internalize those gaps as their definition of love and worth. This chapter explores how a father's presence—or absence—shapes identity and teaches you how to reclaim your sense of security.

Inner Vows and Contracts

Pain doesn't disappear when ignored. It burrows deep, shaping subconscious beliefs and internal agreements you didn't realize you made. These inner vows become a private governing system that controls your choices. This chapter helps you identify and dismantle those contracts so your identity can be freed.

Forgiveness and Letting Go

Emotional pain is heavy—and when it is not properly released, it manifests as stagnation, exhaustion, and even physical symptoms. This chapter walks you through the transformative power of forgiveness—not as a favor to others, but as a pathway to your own freedom.

Boundaries

Unhealed pain often leads to over-giving and under-receiving. This chapter teaches you how to establish and maintain boundaries that protect your time, body, energy, and emotional space—without guilt or fear of rejection.

Transformational Leadership

Many people are leaders by default. Many are the ones that others rely on, confusing consistency with strength, and overlooking their inner battles of self-doubt and imposter syndrome. This chapter equips you with practical assertiveness skills that build confidence and empower you to walk boldly in your leadership identity.

Your Invitation Forward

Now that you have a glimpse of what it means to shatter emotional roadblocks, only one decision remains: *Will you say yes to what's ahead?* This book will ask you to dig deep. To confront pain, you may have learned to survive rather than heal. It will help you peel back layers of labels placed on you by trauma, culture, and experience—revealing the version of you God always intended to emerge.

I often describe healing like the ocean. The intensity of waves shifts with the moon, just as emotions rise and fall throughout the healing process. Some moments will feel overwhelming. Others will be calm and steady. But as you address the pain and apply the tools in these pages, the waters will settle. Now, let's begin. Together, we will mend each emotional space—so you can fully step into your **Real ID**.

Step One

TRANSFORMATIONAL SELF-CARE

Transformational self-care is not indulgence; it is obedience. It is the discipline of leaving environments, mindsets, and attachments that quietly erode your soul—before they consume you. Genesis 19 tells the story of Lot and his family being warned to leave Sodom before its destruction. At first glance, the passage reads as an account of judgment and escape, but at its core, it is a study in what happens when the soul lingers too long in places that God has already declared unsafe. Lot is seated at the city gates– a position of familiarity and influence. Sodom has not only surrounded him; it has shaped him. Even when divine warning arrives, movement is slow. Hesitation replaces urgency, and negotiation replaces obedience. Eventually, the angels must intervene, physically pulling Lot and his family out.

This is often how neglected self-care manifests. Not as rebellion, but as exhaustion. Not as defiance, but as depletion. When the soul is overextended, discernment fades, urgency fades, and the ability to move decisively weakens.

Functioning in Dysfunction

One of the greatest struggles for people who carry multiple roles and responsibilities is recognizing when endurance has replaced health. High-functioning individuals often learn how to survive emotionally unsafe environments without realizing the cost. According to the World Health Organization (WHO), the prevalence of anxiety and depression increased 25 percent. This surge did not create new dysfunction; it revealed existing patterns. When routines collapsed, and distractions disappeared, many were forced to confront unresolved grief, fear, and emotional pain–often without the internal tools necessary to process them.

Like Lot, many had grown accustomed to living in what was quietly destroying them. As a mental health professional, I have often encountered individuals who did not identify their struggles as a dysfunction. They had learned how to function comfortably within it. Sodom did not fall overnight. It deteriorated slowly until destruction became inevitable. Self-care becomes essential when familiar coping mechanisms can no longer shield the soul from collapse.

Transformational Self-Care as Divine Intervention

The World Health Organization defines self-care as the ability to maintain health and cope with illness with or without professional support. While accurate, this definition addresses survival not transformation. Transformational self-care is the intentional practice of giving your mind, body, and soul the specific, healthy interventions they require, at the moment they are needed–without guilt or self-condemnation. It is not reactive; it is responsive. It requires listening inward before damage becomes irreversible. Lot is urged repeatedly to leave. Delay proves dangerous. Likewise, when emotional, mental, or spiritual warning signs go unaddressed, the soul begins negotiating for familiarity rather than safety.

The Danger of Small Thinking

When Lot finally agrees to flee, he refuses the mountains—the place of refuge—and requests a smaller city called Zoar. Its name means *small, insignificant, few*. God allows it, but the symbolism is sobering: **trauma shrinks vision**. When the soul has endured prolonged stress, pain, or fear, it often settles for what feels manageable rather than what is divinely appointed. Small thinking feels safer than faith when emotional reserves are depleted. Lot eventually leaves Zoar anyway, ending up isolated in a cave—proof that temporary compromise never produces lasting refuge. Transformational self-care restores the capacity to trust God beyond survival mode.

Looking Back and Becoming Immobilized

Lot's wife offers one of Scripture's most haunting images. As she looks back toward Sodom, she becomes a pillar of salt. This moment is often framed solely as disobedience, but symbolically, it reveals the cost of emotional attachment to former places of comfort—even when those places were destructive. Salt is meant to be spread. It preserves and enhances. A pillar, however, is fixed. Immobile. Unable to move forward or pour outward. When the soul remains anchored to the past, influence diminishes. Energy drains. Identity stagnates.

Neglecting self-care does not merely slow progress—it immobilizes purpose. Looking back does not preserve what was lost; it forfeits what could be built.

Emotional Health and the Unattended Soul

Emotional health reflects one's ability to recognize, regulate, and respond to emotions. Emotions themselves are not harmful; suppression and neglect are. Emotional pain that is ignored often relocates into the body, manifesting as chronic stress, illness, or unexplained fatigue. When emotional wounds remain untreated, they deepen. Attachment wounds rooted in rejection or abandonment can evolve into identity fractures when left unaddressed. Delayed healing compounds damage. Like Sodom, unhealed emotional environments do not remain neutral—they deteriorate.

The Soul as the True Battleground

Scripture uses the terms *heart* and *soul* interchangeably. In Hebrew thought, the heart encompasses the inner being: mind, will, emotions, and lived experiences. What psychology calls emotional and mental health; Scripture identifies as soul care. Leader of the *Soul Healing Movement*, Dr.

Joshua P. Smith, captures this clearly with the following statement: *"We are spiritual beings, living in a physical body, doing life from our soul."* Identity flows from the soul, and pain distorts identity when care is neglected.

This is why Scripture instructs:

"Above all else, guard your heart, for everything you do flows from it."— *Proverbs 4:23 (NIV)*

Transformational self-care is the act of guarding what determines direction, discernment, and destiny.

Rest, Resistance, and Preservation

Jesus modeled withdrawal and rest—not because He lacked strength, but because rest preserves clarity. Exhaustion clouds judgment. Overextension weakens resolve. A worn-down soul hesitates when it should move. The enemy does not need to destroy you if he can simply exhaust you. Self-care is resistance against spiritual erosion. It preserves timing, strengthens discernment, and prevents missed seasons.

Pouring Without Losing Your Oil

Lot's wife lost her influence because she was immobilized by the past. Transformational self-care reverses this pattern. It teaches proper order: **care for the soul first so that what flows outward remains life-giving**. You cannot lead well from depletion. You cannot pour endlessly without consequence. Seasons require discernment, not self-neglect.

Moving Forward Without Shrinking

Lot had to be pulled out of Sodom. Transformational self-care ensures that you do not require rescue from what you were warned to leave. It cultivates the awareness, strength, and courage to move when God says move–without hesitation, without shrinking, without looking back. This is not self-indulgence; it is stewardship. This is how you leave what destroys you and guard what sustains you.

Transformational self-care requires courage—the courage to stop shrinking, stop minimizing, and stop silencing your needs. Confidence grows when you honor your limits, recognize your triggers, and respond with self-awareness rather than self-betrayal. When you learn to listen to your body, acknowledge emotional responses, and address patterns honestly, healing deepens. Power is reclaimed. Your voice is restored. You do not move forward by holding onto what God has already released you from. You move forward by caring for the life He is actively preserving.

Transformational self-care is the practice of guarding your heart, honoring your limits, restoring your soul, and stewarding your energy so that you can move forward without shrinking, settling, or becoming stuck. It is choosing obedience over exhaustion, discernment over guilt, and growth over comfort. It is how you protect your oil, preserve your influence, and step fully into the future God has prepared for you.

Step Two

HEALING FROM MOTHER WOUNDS

Let me forewarn you: this is where the rubber meets the road. As an African American woman from South Mississippi, I was taught from birth to respect my elders—without question, without hesitation. In many Southern families, there is a "Big Mama" or "Madear"—the matriarch whose presence anchors the entire lineage. Her words carry weight. Her sacrifices are honored. Her authority is rarely challenged. This reverence is deeply cultural, shaped in part by the legacy of slavery. When enslaved men were torn from their families and sold to distant plantations, they were not only physically separated—they were systematically emasculated. Their strength was perceived as a threat. Their leadership was intentionally dismantled. In their absence, women became the stabilizing force within fractured households. They carried children, grief, responsibility, and survival on their backs.

Generations later, that resilience is still honored. In many communities, mothers are revered because they have to be everything. And rightfully so—mothers are foundational to the health and stability of a family. Their presence (or absence) shapes identity, attachment, and emotional safety in ways few relationships ever will.

However, here is the tension. Not everyone can say the word *"mother"* and feel warmth. For some, that word triggers confusion, grief, anger, or even silence. If you were to be honest, some of the struggles you face in your parenting, romantic relationships, and even your relationship with God are tethered to wounds inflicted by the very person whose touch was meant to nurture you, but hurt you instead. That truth is uncomfortable. But healing requires honesty. The reality is, some of who you are becoming is because of your mother, and some of who you must become will be in spite of her.

As children, many of us silently rehearsed painful conclusions long before we had the emotional language to question them:

"My mama didn't love me."

"She loved my siblings more than me."

"She was softer with them but harder on me."

"She gave me away but kept them."

These weren't dramatic declarations spoken aloud. They were quiet interpretations formed in developing minds trying to make sense of inconsistent love. Those inner whispers became identity statements. You may have had a mother who listened attentively to everyone else but dismissed your voice. You may have felt invisible or grown up as a girl in a family where boys were favored. You may have even grown up in a home where emotional instability dictated the atmosphere or where addiction, depression, volatility, or silence filled rooms that should have felt safe. If your mother came home intoxicated, high, or emotionally unraveling, you may have become the stabilizer. You tucked her into bed. YOU cooked meals. YOU protected younger siblings. YOU read the room before speaking. You were not allowed to simply be a child. You became her caretaker and parent.

When a child is forced to parent their parent, something inside them fractures. Not because they lacked strength—but because they were carrying weight their nervous system was never designed to bear. That fracture doesn't disappear with adulthood. It follows you into friendships, marriages, leadership, and ministry. It shapes how you attach, how you respond to conflict, how you perceive correction, and how you define love. This chapter is not about dishonoring mothers. It is about confronting the impact of unmet needs so that they no longer unconsciously control your life. You cannot heal what you refuse to name, and you cannot fully become who God created you to be while protecting the wounds that shaped you.

Generational Trauma: A Family Story

In my line of work, I hear many stories. One that stood out to me was from a grandparent who was reflecting on caring for her grandchildren.

"I had to raise them kids. Their mama would run off chasing after a man and leave them alone for weeks. No food, no care. I couldn't let Child

Protective Services take them, so they stayed with me."

In that moment, everything about their family dynamics clicked. I understood why the siblings were so tightly bonded to one another. Their survival depended on it. They learned early that they couldn't trust their mother to stay. Their sibling bond was also a manifestation of their fear of being abandoned. Following the conversation, I began to take a deeper look and empathized with the mother. Her behavior wasn't random. Perhaps she was chasing after something she never received—safety, validation, and love.

As I traced the family's behavior, patterns emerged. The grandmother shared her story of growing up with parents who were both substance abusers. This led to her caring for her siblings and figuring out life, alone. Though her parents were physically present, their emotional absence impacted how she mothered her own children. This is the tragedy of generational trauma: **wounded mothers often wound their children.**

The Legacy of the Mother Wound

From these cycles flow a thousand unspoken messages that shape how daughters see themselves. You may recognize some of these:

"My mother doesn't approve of me."

"I'll never be good enough."

"I have to look perfect, act perfect, and keep it all together."

"If she doesn't love me, no one else will."

When a child internalizes rejection, it grows into low self-esteem, comparison, imposter syndrome, and perfectionism in adulthood.

Comparison whispers, *"Everyone else is loved and chosen, but not me."*

Imposter syndrome says, *"If I step out, they'll all see what's wrong with me."*

Perfectionism insists, *"If I can just become flawless, maybe she'll finally accept me."*

People-pleasing pleads, *"If I bend myself into who she wants me to be, maybe I'll be loved."*

Over time, these survival strategies become false identities. You begin shaving off pieces of yourself, hiding parts of your personality, and presenting only the "palatable" version that might finally earn her approval. But here's the truth: **it was never about you not being enough. It was about her wounds, not your worth.**

Understanding the Mother Wound

The mother wound occurs when a mother (or mother figure) fails to provide the love, safety, and affirmation her child needs to thrive. Sometimes it is obvious—abandonment, rejection, or neglect. Other times, it's subtle. A mother may meet your physical needs but remain emotionally unavailable. She may feed you, clothe you, and ensure you look nice for the world, but when you cry, hurt, or long for comfort, she isn't there. The wound is formed not only by *what happened*, but often by *what didn't happen*.

A mother's role is to:

- Offer unconditional love and acceptance.
- Nurture and provide emotional safety.
- Model self-worth and identity.
- Guide her children into maturity with empathy and consistency.

When these needs go unmet—through criticism, absence, addiction, abuse, or even emotional fragility—the child grows up with an internalized message: *I am not wanted. I am not safe. I am not enough.*

When Pain Speaks

I will never forget the year two thousand and twenty. Life had already stretched me to my breaking point—my marriage was fragile, I was in therapy, and my identity felt scattered between roles of mother, wife, work, and serving at my church. My therapist began pressing me toward a truth I quietly had been resisting. I had outsourced my worth to everyone else and didn't know how to validate myself outside of the roles I filled or the organizations I served at. I continued therapy for another year, doing some much-needed inner healing and identity work. I'd come to a place in my life where I was able to self-validate and place boundaries around my roles.

Within a year's time, my life drastically changed. My healing journey was complete, or so I thought. The following year, I attended a leadership conference. One of the guest speakers—who moves powerfully in prophecy, healing, and deliverance—

prayed over us. When she reached me, she leaned close and whispered words I didn't expect:

"Your mother didn't want you."

A scream tore out of me, a sound I had never heard come from my own body. It was grief, rejection, and abandonment all at once. My body knew it before my mind admitted it. I had lived with the ache of feeling unwanted my entire life. Although my mother had given me away to be adopted, and though I had been raised by my aunt, who loved me well, that primal wound never fully closed.

Deliverance began for me that night, but healing took years after that. It started with my journaling about how I truly felt about her. I'd gone most of my life avoiding facing the pain of abandonment and rejection despite its residue interwoven in my being. I knew that if I were to truly heal, I had to come face-to-face with the pain of it. I remember it like it was yesterday. I was sitting in my living room. I began to write out all of the feelings about her that I'd been repressing. I felt every emotion in the book. My handwriting changed with each expression of emotion. By the end of that session, I felt lighter and the weight of pain lessened.

As my healing journey progressed, God began dealing with me about my heart towards her. The pain may have come from someone else, but you are responsible for the healing. God began to show me who my mother really was. I stopped seeing her as a woman who wounded me and began seeing her as an 18-year-old girl who was afraid, lost, and doing her best to survive on her own despite her own traumas. I began seeing her as a woman who once had dreams of her own, but whose life struggles stole them from her. I stopped interpreting her actions as rejection and started seeing her as a woman who loved me enough to accept that, in the state she was in, lacked the capacity to give me what I needed, which, to me, is what true motherhood is: unselfishness.

With each eye-opening realization came a softening and tenderness in my heart toward her. Love and mercy began pouring from my heart, along with deep gratitude for her choosing the gift of adoption over the finality of abortion. Because of that choice, she is truly one of the main reasons I am here today.

Signs of the Mother Wound

The mother wound can take many forms. Here are some of the most common patterns:

1. **Physical provision without emotional presence:** You were fed, clothed, and housed, but your emotions were invisible.
2. **Rejection during vulnerable moments:** Instead of comfort when you cried, you heard: *"Get up. You're fine. Stop being dramatic."*
3. **Criticism instead of affirmation:** You were told you could never do anything right. Anger and harsh words replaced nurture.
4. **Role reversal:** You were expected to meet your mother's emotional needs—becoming her confidant, friend, or even parent—while your needs went unmet.
5. **Generational or environmental trauma:** Poverty, addiction, untreated mental illness, or abuse created a context where your mother couldn't be emotionally safe.
6. **Modeling dysfunction:** Instead of teaching healthy expression, some mothers encourage fighting, aggression, or unhealthy coping mechanisms.

In every scenario, the result is the same: the child learns that *I cannot rely on my mother for safety, affirmation, or emotional presence.*

The Impact of the Mother Wound

The effects of mother wounds show up in adulthood in countless ways:

- Low self-worth and people-pleasing
- Difficulty setting boundaries
- Self-sabotaging beliefs ("I am not enough," "I am unlovable")
- Triggers in relationships, especially intimate ones
- Challenges with trust and vulnerability

Many don't know that these effects are there until something triggers them. Triggers can be **emotional** (anxious, heaviness, wanting to isolate for protection), **physical** (tension, heart beating fast, or sweating when interacting or the thought of interacting with your mother), or **mental** (replay of negative words or action from your mother). Each trigger is a signal pointing back to an unhealed place.

God's Design vs. Wounded Reality

God designed mothers to be the first example of nurture, empathy, and identity. But sin, brokenness, and trauma interrupt that design. Some mothers were themselves carrying wounds from their mothers, perpetuating cycles of rejection and pain. For women of color, these cycles often trace back to generational trauma as far-reaching as slavery, poverty, and systemic oppression.

Here's the truth: God never wastes a wound. Even the deepest maternal rejection does not erase His plan. He placed you in environments—whether through adoptive families, mentors, spiritual mothers, or communities—that could still prepare you for His purpose.

The Fear of Becoming Her

One of the greatest fears women with mother wounds carry is this: *"I don't want to be like my mom."* This fear often fuels people-pleasing. This often leads you to overcompensate by being endlessly positive, overly accommodating, or hyper-vigilant about your children's needs. This fear can also lead you to become the opposite of your mother. This underlying fear serves one purpose: to trick you into losing your real identity by focusing on your mother's perceived identity. Transformation is not about swinging from one extreme to another. It's about becoming the whole, healed version of who **God designed you to be.**

Renouncing False Identities

Healing begins when you make the choice to come out of agreement with the false identities you took on for survival. These are not who you are.

- Perfectionism is not your personality.
- Fear is not your personality.
- Hyper-independence is not your personality.
- People-pleasing is not your personality.

These are personas created out of pain. But God is calling you back to your true identity—His daughter. Take a moment to declare:

"I renounce every false identity I took on because of my wounds. I come out of agreement with every persona rooted in fear, rejection, or trauma. I receive my true identity as God's beloved daughter."

Begin the Healing

Healing the mother's wound doesn't mean ignoring what happened. It means facing it with God's presence, telling the truth about it, and learning how to replace old narratives with affirming truths rooted in Scripture. Here are some practical ways to begin walking out this freedom:

Name The Wound

Give yourself permission to say: *"My mother was not emotionally safe."*

Recognize The Patterns

Identify how that wound shows up in your triggers, relationships, or self-talk.

Rewrite The Narrative

Replace lies of rejection with God's truth: *"I am chosen. I am wanted. I am loved."*

Seek Safe Spaces to Grow

Healing often requires therapy, community, or mentors who can model the nurture you missed.

Practice Self-Care and Healthy Boundaries

Protecting your healing journey means refusing to re-expose yourself to harm without wisdom and limits.

Maintaining The Healing

Practice new responses

If your mother is still living, prepare how you'll respond when triggered. No more shrinking back or exploding in anger. Choose firm, assertive, respectful communication.

Develop an emotional self-care plan

When you feel triggered, know what you will do—journal, pray, step away, or call a trusted friend. Don't wait until the moment of crisis to figure it out.

Set healthy boundaries

Boundaries are not disrespectful. Saying "no" is not dishonor. Protecting your peace is not rebellion. It's wisdom.

Reject guilt and manipulation

Some mothers will try to pull you back into the role of the obedient child who never questions or challenges. Resist that pull. You are not who you were—you are healing and growing.

Stay in community

Healing is not meant to be done alone. Share your process with safe people who can encourage, pray, and remind you of the truth when the lies feel louder.

Healing the mother's wound is not about dishonoring your mother. It is about reclaiming the parts of yourself that were buried beneath trauma, rejection, and unmet needs. It is about coming into agreement with who God says you are—and stepping out of agreement with every lie that says otherwise. You are not destined to repeat the cycles of your bloodline. You are called to break them. If you have made it this far, I'm proud of you. The journey continues as we step into the next chapter: **Healing Father Wounds.**

Step Three

HEALING FROM FATHER WOUNDS

Fathers are a child's first introduction to masculinity and often the first lens through which we interpret God. They impart belonging, model protection, establish identity, and cultivate confidence for daughters. Even something as simple as roughhousing — playful wrestling, tossing in the air, mock competition — has been shown to build resilience and internal security in children. It teaches them, "You can fall and recover. You can engage the world and remain safe." What happens when that foundation is missing? What happens when a father is absent — physically or emotionally? What happens when he is present in body but unavailable in spirit?

As I write this, I see an image: a crowded waiting room. People everywhere. The room is noisy, busy, and filled with activity. However, there is one person sitting in the middle of it all—completely alone. That is what father absence feels like. You move through rooms, enter relationships, and transition through seasons, yet internally, you feel like you are winging it. The self-security that was supposed to be anchored early never fully formed.

In addition to providing security, fathers also impart identity. One of the most profound revelations God gave me about father wounds came from two moments in Scripture — two decrees that were issued by kings to kill newborn boys. The first one appears in Exodus:

"When you serve as midwife to the Hebrew women... if it is a son, you shall kill him..."— *Exodus 1:15–17* **(English Standard Version)**

Pharaoh, threatened by the multiplication of Israel, ordered the death of male infants. The second appears in Matthew:

*"Herod… sent and killed all the male children in Bethlehem… two years old or under."— Matthew 2:13–16 (**ESV**)*

Each decree is made by different kings from different eras, but somehow the strategy remains the same, to attach identity at its source. In Exodus, Israel was in bondage. Pharaoh represents oppression—the systemic stripping of dignity, agency, and identity. But whenever bondage intensifies in Scripture, deliverance is near. In Matthew, Herod attempted to intercept Jesus' destiny, but because of His parents' obedience, Jesus was preserved. The enemy's tactics are consistent: if you can kill identity early, you can delay purpose. Fathers are pillars in families and communities. When they are stable, identity and purpose stabilize. When they are fractured, identity and purpose fractures.

*"…but the people who know their God will be strong and take action."— Daniel 11:32 (**Good News Translation**)*

Identity produces strength, and Strength produces action. When identity is unclear, confidence wavers.

Boundaries blur. Self-doubt grows loud. Psychologically, father wounds refer to the emotional pain that stems from a strained, absent, inconsistent, or abusive paternal relationship. Research consistently affirms what Scripture already implies: the father-child dynamic significantly impacts emotional development.

Father wounds often stem from:

- **Emotional neglect** — absence of affirmation, protection, or connection
- **Physical absence or unavailability** — divorce, abandonment, preoccupation
- **Abuse** — physical, verbal, or emotional harm
- **Unrealistic expectations** — criticism that breeds inadequacy
- **Dysfunctional modeling** — unhealthy communication, anger, instability

Without healing, these wounds do not stay contained, they project. You will begin projecting unmet needs onto other men and onto God. When I first became a believer, I was passionate and committed, but whenever I made a mistake, I would struggle with accepting forgiveness. I had an underlying fear that God's love would be withdrawn when I was "bad." That fear was not theological. It was relational. My biological father's love had felt inconsistent. And without realizing it, I assumed all male love — even divine love — functioned the same way.

In September 2024, I had a dream that confronted this directly. In the dream, two sisters were sharing testimonies of overcoming childhood trauma. A woman in the audience stood up, visibly shaken, yelling that she could relate. Her voice carried deep pain. The scene then shifted to a scene where the same young lady was now lying in a bed, undergoing deliverance. I called out for help from my friend that was with me (This friend is also called into the ministry of healing and deliverance).

She responded,

"I need to use the bathroom first."

I waited but she never returned. I searched the house looking for her. Each room that I entered was clean, empty, and dark.

When I woke up, the Holy Spirit began revealing its meaning. He shared that this dream exposed that though I had experienced freedom in parts of my life, I'd not experienced full restoration in other parts due to some underlying fears. As a result, my identity from the abandonment and neglect of my father, had not yet been fully rebuilt and was manifesting itself in my life as self-doubt and low self-worth. Freedom is not the same as fullness. It is not enough to be set free from wounds. If you do not intentionally fill the empty space, anything can occupy it. Healing requires replacement. You must fill that space with truth, light, the Word, and with intentional restoration — or old patterns will return wearing new faces.

The Impact of Father Wounds on Women

Many people will go through their entire lives and not stop to pay attention to the impact that these wounds are having on their beliefs about themselves, the world around them, and their interactions with the people they encounter from day-to-day. However, these wounds are what are showing up in the world. They are what lead you to question the decisions you make and second-guess your success. It is also what's whispering to you to scan the rooms you enter, wondering if others see your flaws. What began as unmet needs in childhood is slowly becoming your silent (but loud) internal critic.

Emotional and Psychological Effects

- Low self-esteem
- Chronic feelings of inadequacy
- Imposter syndrome
- Fear of rejection

Relational Patterns

Attachment theory teaches that early caregiver relationships shape later intimacy patterns. When a father is absent or inconsistent, daughters often internalize distorted lessons about love. Two core lessons fathers are meant to impart are: **self-security** (confidence in oneself and trust in others) and **identity** (clarity about who you are and what you deserve).

When these important elements are missing, love can become intertwined with anxiety or avoidance. Some women become anxiously attached, clingy, over-giving, and have a strong fear of abandonment. Others swing to the opposite extreme by becoming emotionally avoidant of anything that could expose them to hurt, including fearing intimacy. There are some that oscillate between both— intensely attached until they sense withdrawal, then abruptly detached to avoid rejection. At the core of each behavior pattern is the same wound: "If they leave, I am not enough."

Behavioral Impact

- Seeking validation externally
- Overdependence or emotional isolation
- Difficulty establishing boundaries

Spiritual Impact

Perhaps most subtly, father wounds distort one's perception of God. If your earthly father was inconsistent, distant, harsh, or absent, it may feel unnatural to view God as steady, protective, and safe. You may love Him, but struggle to trust Him.

Begin The Healing

Acknowledge and Accept

- Name the wound.
- Acknowledge the impact.

- Validate your feelings without minimizing them. Denial preserves pain. Naming it begins dismantling it.

Reflect and Release

Therapeutic journaling will help you get to the root of the wound and release the pain attached to it.

- What *unmet needs did I have as a child?*
- *How have these wounds shaped my beliefs about myself, men, and God?*

Then confront forgiveness. Forgiveness is not justification. It is liberation. Releasing your father from the debt you feel he owes you does not excuse what happened — it frees you from carrying it.

Rebuild and Redefine

Healing is not only subtraction. It is reconstruction. Affirmations help to replace negative thoughts and beliefs associated with the wounds wile boundaries help you maintain your healing work.

Identity Affirmations

- I am loved.
- I am worthy.

- I am enough.
- My past does not define my future.

Boundary Work

- Define what healthy love looks like.
- Identify what you will no longer tolerate.
- Choose relationships aligned with truth, not trauma.

Here's the deeper truth: Your father may have shaped your introduction to identity, but he does not get to define your destiny. God is not the projection of your pain. He is the restorer of what was fractured.

Reconnect Spiritually

Invite God to heal father wounds and fill emotional gaps by using scripture-based affirmations such as this one:

"A father to the fatherless, a defender of widows, is God in his holy dwelling." Psalm 68:5 (NIV)

Seek Support

Seek professional counseling or therapy. You can also join supportive communities or accountability groups like our eight-week program, Healed University, for extra support.

Step Four

BREAKING INNER VOWS AND SPIRITUAL CONTRACTS

The first vow I ever made wasn't spoken in a church. It wasn't written down. It wasn't announced to anyone. It was whispered in the quiet chambers of my heart the moment I realized something painful: Love can leave, people can change, and safety is not guaranteed. Without even knowing I was doing it; I made an agreement with my own fear: *"I will never let anyone hurt me like that again."* Maybe you've made one too. Not out loud. Not formally. But internally. A vow that sounded like wisdom… but was actually self-protection. Because that's what inner vows are: They are the promises we make in pain that quietly shape the rest of our lives.

When Boundaries Become Brick Walls

On the surface, inner vows can look a lot like boundaries. We live in a generation where healing language is everywhere. Self-love is celebrated. Cutting people off is normalized. "Protect your peace" is the anthem. And sometimes, those things are necessary. But if we're honest, a lot of what we call boundaries today are actually bruises. Unhealed disappointments dressed up as empowerment. We all know someone with a strong cut-off game, right? The moment things get uncomfortable, they disappear. The moment vulnerability is required, they retreat. The moment intimacy asks for softness, they harden. It feels like strength, but it's often a sign of something deeper—An unhealed soul trying not to bleed again.

What Are Inner Vows?

Inner vows are subconscious promises you make to yourself after your trust has been violated. They form after betrayal. After abandonment. After trauma. After disappointment. After the kind of heartbreak that changes how you see people and how you see yourself. Inner vows often sound like:

"I will never need anyone again."

"I won't ever be vulnerable."

"No one can be trusted."

"I'll always have to do it myself."

"Love is dangerous."

"People always leave."

Here's what makes them so powerful: your mind believes what you repeat; your spirit responds to what you agree with; and your life follows what you declare. Inner vows don't just live in your thoughts. They build invisible brick walls around your heart. Walls that serve two purposes: To keep people out and to keep you from being loved well.

Maybe You've Made One Too

Maybe you didn't call it a vow. Maybe you called it maturity or wisdom. Maybe you labeled it as 'learning a lesson'. On the surface, people see you as confident and a master at setting boundaries. In reality, there are some underlying thoughts and beliefs guarding your heart and influencing your actions. If you were to peel back the band-aid of your subconscious, it would reveal wounds such as:

I'm better off alone.

Friendships don't last anyway.

Men can't be trusted.

I won't ever depend on anyone.

I won't let myself feel that deeply again.

That isn't confidence. That's survival, and survival always has a cost. Inner vows may protect you from pain, but they also block you from freedom. They don't just keep hurt out; they keep healing out too.

Inner vows steal:

- Emotional intimacy
- Healthy love
- Softness
- Trust
- Connection
- Rest
- Receiving

Without intervention, the vow that kept you safe at 12 will keep you stuck at 42. What began as a means of protection from pain, hurt, abuse, and/or neglect will eventually become the very thing that leads to your emotional imprisonment.

How Inner Vows Are Formed

I remember a season in college when I dated a particular guy on and off from undergrad to graduate school. In the last year of my graduate program, I began going to therapy and doing the hard work of facing my trauma. We'd entered another serious but not-so-serious phase of the relationship. But something in me couldn't fully relax. On one hand, the relationship felt familiar, while underneath the surface, I couldn't ignore the fear I felt about being with this individual.

One night, I decided I needed answers. I curled up on my couch with a blanket and my journal. Writing has always been where I tell the truth. I started listing the pros and cons, but nothing surfaced. I then started mapping our relationship cycle — because all behavior moves in patterns. Therapists Susan Johnson and Leslie Greenberg calls these cycles "the relationship dance." They taught that these dances are often driven by attachment wounds which occurred during childhood but ultimately, governs adult relationships.

As I traced our dance, something surfaced. My fear of rejection was dominating everything. Not because he was rejecting me, but because I was already expecting it. I realized I wasn't responding to him. I was responding to my history. I had experienced abandonment long before I ever met him, and as a result, had formed inner vows that were hindering me in that relationship. He to, had abandonment wounds of his own. We weren't only dating each other; we were triggering each other's pain. We came together through familiarity, but couldn't fully connect because of the underlying fears. Inner wounds lead to inner promises, and those inner promises become inner vows.

Common Inner Vows

The Independence Vow— *"I don't need anyone."*

The Distrust Vow— *"People always leave."*

The Overachiever Vow— *"If I'm perfect, I won't be rejected."*

The Numbing Vow— "I won't feel too deeply again."

The Control Vow— *"If I stay in charge, I won't get hurt."*

The Scarcity Vow— *"Just enough is all I can expect."*
You won't be able to heal what you can't identify. So, let me ask you: Which one have you been living under?

Inner Vows Become Spiritual Contracts

Here's the part many people miss: Inner vows don't just affect emotions. They create agreements, and agreements have spiritual weight.

Scripture warns us:

"It is better not to make a vow than to make one and not fulfill it."— Ecclesiastes 5:4–6 (NIV)

Contracts demand fulfillment–even the ones you made in pain. Inner vows become spiritual contracts when they create open doors for bitterness, fear, and limitation to take root. Pain left unhealed becomes permission for the enemy to come in and wreak havoc in your soul.

What Are Spiritual Contracts?

Spiritual contracts are legally binding agreements made in the spirit realm through unhealed emotional pain. They are not spooky. They are not mystical. They are simply the beliefs you partnered with when you were bleeding. Contracts like:

"I will always struggle."

"God helps others, not me."

"I don't deserve more than this."

"This is as good as it gets."

"I'll never be chosen."

Isaiah calls them breaches:

> "You will be called the Repairer of Broken Walls…" — Isaiah 58:12 (**NIV**)

The Kingdom is legal, and the enemy is a legalist. Satan cannot destroy your destiny without agreement. That's why the serpent's first strategy in Eden was not to attack. It was to doubt if God really said what He said. We have to remember that the enemy's number one goal is always agreement.

How to Break Inner Vows and Contracts

The next few steps are your roadmap to breaking inner vows and contracts. Healing requires more than awareness. It requires release. Release may come in many stages. You may experience instant relief, while for more deep-rooted issues, your release may come over time. I am a firm believer that God will show you the areas of your heart that have been broken at the time that you are mature enough to walk through the healing.

Acknowledge the Root

Once you recognize the fruit, you can find the root. Where did this vow begin? This step is the foundation by which your healing will begin and is one that you should not take lightly. Which is also why you CANNOT afford to sugar coat what has happened to you. This is not the time for you to protect the reputation or ego of the people who may be connected to your wounds.

Validate What You Need

What did the younger version of you need? This part is vital because you have to admit that you may have needed something that others were not emotionally capable of providing for you. Ask yourself, "Did I need… Safety? Love? Protection?" Be honest with yourself. This may be the first time that you've ever had to validate your pain, so it may be emotional. If it becomes too overwhelming for you, pause and use some emotional grounding exercises and deep breathing to help you through.

Break Legal Access

Pain creates permission slips while healing revokes them. The enemy is a legalist. If you have given him legal grounds to operate in your life, he will continue to do so until the contract is broken. However, the good news is that God is also a legalist. He honors His Word. When we come before the courts of heaven and present the case that the enemy has no legal authority to continue making you pay for vows and contracts that you made, He has no choice but to grant your petition.

Denounce

Declare that you are making these vows out of pain, was wrong, and that they were made as a result of the pain that you've encountered

Renounce

Abandon the agreements made my coming out of agreement with the lies of pain and into agreement with God's says about you or about the situation.

Forgive and Invite Healing

There is no real healing without forgiveness. Forgiveness is not a feeling; it is an act of faith and obedience. Some people or situations will be easier to forgive than others, but you have to walk through this step regardless of how painful it may be. I strongly encourage doing this with someone you trust like an accountability partner, mentor, therapist, or spiritual leader. The hardest person for most people to forgive is themselves. This is because a lot of people carry a great deal of guilt and shame about what has happened to them in their lives. This is often false self-accusations as much of what happened to you was not your fault nor would it had been your choice. We'll talk more about healing and forgiveness in the next chapter. Ask God to heal the wounds beneath the vow.

Inner Vow Healing Activation

Journaling

The vow I made was: ___________

I made it after experiencing: ___________

It has cost me: ___________

Today, I release the agreement that says:

____

God's truth over my life is: ___________

A Prayer of Release

Father,

I repent for every vow I made in pain. I cancel every agreement with fear, rejection, abandonment, and scarcity. I renounce the lie that I must stay guarded to stay safe. Heal the wounded places in me that still expect betrayal. Restore softness. Restore trust. Restore freedom. In Jesus' name.

Amen.

Survival is not your destiny. Inner vows are not proof that you're broken. They are proof that you survived. But survival is not where your story ends. The wall was never your identity. It was only your attempt to stay safe, and now, God is inviting you to live uncontracted. Unbound. Unwounded. Whole.

Step Five

FORGIVENESS AND LETTING GO

One of the greatest barriers to healing and discovering your Real ID is the burden of dead weight. Bitterness, resentment, anger, and unforgiveness can be heavy emotions. These heavy emotions, rooted in your past experiences, don't just sit quietly in the background; they actively anchor you in a sea of misery— a misery you are unintentionally sustaining by refusing to release. It's not easy. Anyone who tells you otherwise is simply wrong. It won't be easy, but it is necessary. If you truly want to excel — to heal — to step fully into your purpose — you must learn to release what was never yours to carry. In this chapter, we'll explore the transformative power of forgiveness — not just toward others, but toward yourself. You'll learn how to release resentment, anger, and pain, and experience the emotional freedom that only forgiveness can provide.

Forgiveness Is Not Optional for Healing

When you've walked through deep hurt, betrayal, or disappointment, forgiveness may feel impossible. In fact, some will argue that you don't need to forgive in order to heal. I don't agree with that school of thought. Biologically, spiritually, and emotionally — we were never designed to carry prolonged bitterness. There have been studies that have shown that unresolved trauma contributes to disease, weakens the immune system, disrupts sleep, elevates blood pressure, and invites chronic stress into the body.

Scripture affirms this truth:

"Let all bitterness and wrath and anger and clamor and slander be put away from you, along with all malice. Be kind to one another, tenderhearted, forgiving one another, as God in Christ forgave you." — Ephesians 4:31-32 (**ESV**)

Forgiveness is not about letting anyone off the hook — it's about removing yourself from a hook you were never meant to be tethered to.

The Hardest Person to Forgive

Often, the most difficult person to forgive isn't someone else—it's forgiving yourself. The regret over the choices we made. The shame we carry for not seeing the red flags sooner. The guilt for staying too long or allowing things to happen that should have been stopped. Self-forgiveness is one of the most courageous acts of healing. Without it, we stay bound not only to what others have done but to our own internal accusations.

The Cliffside Encounter

I remember sitting in my very first graduate class studying marriage and family therapy when my professor shared a powerful story about forgiveness. He described a woman, much like many of us, who was walking her own path toward healing. She was determined to reclaim what had been lost — to gather the broken pieces of her life and move forward. Along her journey, she encountered someone sitting alone on the edge of a cliff. Curious, she stopped and they began to talk.

"Where are you headed?" the person asked.

"I'm on a journey to heal," she answered. *"To find life. To understand my purpose—and to finally claim all the things I feel I've missed."*

She returned the question. *"And you, where are you going?"*

The person paused, almost indifferent. *"Nowhere, really. I'm just here passing time and enjoying the view."*

Then, without warning, the person handed her a rope. *"Hold this for me."*

The woman took hold instinctively—and as she did, the person jumped off the cliff, leaving her clutching the rope, their life now literally hanging in her hands.

She stood there, stunned. Moments ago, they were talking. Now, she held their fate. If she moved forward on her journey, she would drop the rope— and the person would fall. But if she stayed, she would sacrifice her own healing to hold on. This is where many of us find ourselves: standing at the crossroads.

Do I keep holding onto someone else's choices?
Do I stop my own healing to save them?
Or do I release the rope they freely handed me and allow them to take responsibility for their life?

Let's have an honest look. If someone hands you their rope, they've already made a decision. It's deeply unfair to place that responsibility on you. Now, the decision is yours. Sometimes it feels *impossible* to let go, especially when what you're holding onto is tied to betrayal, abandonment, or wounds inflicted by people who were supposed to love and protect you. This is where forgiveness begins.

Forgiveness: The Prerequisite for Healing

Forgiveness is never easy. It's not easy when the pain comes from people who should have been your safe place. It's not easy when those who hurt you refuse to acknowledge the pain they caused. And it's certainly not easy when well-meaning voices around you simply say, *"You just need to forgive and move on."* While forgiveness is hard, it's necessary.

Matthew 6:14-15 (**ESV**) tells us plainly:

"For if you forgive others their trespasses, your heavenly Father will also forgive you. But if you do not forgive others their trespasses, neither will your Father forgive your trespasses."

I vividly remember a moment early in my marriage. Our marriage was a wreck—no sugarcoating it. One day, I was home alone, angry, and venting to God. "Lord, he won't do this. He won't do that. Why did you give me this man?" I was furiously making the bed, pulling the covers tight, frustrated beyond words. Then the Holy Spirit whispered to my spirit:

"You need to forgive him. Because if you don't, I won't forgive you."

I froze.

"Wait! We're not talking about me right now, God. We're talking about him," I replied.

God wasn't concerned about fixing my husband. He was concerned about fixing my heart. If I were going to step into the calling that He placed on my life, my heart had to be purified first. Your healing and calling will never outpace your willingness to forgive.

Unforgiveness Is Dead Weight

That rope you're holding? That's what unforgiveness feels like. It's dead weight. And the longer you carry it, the more it slows you down. You may still be moving—but you're dragging something that was never yours to carry. The night before I was scheduled to teach this lesson on forgiveness to my Healed University Community, God showed me an example of this in a dream. In the dream, someone I knew was carrying a lifeless body, but threw the body into the trash. It was a harsh image, but a vivid illustration of the importance of discarding emotional dead weight. If you don't discard it, you will end up carrying death into places where God wants to birth life. Let me break it down even further.

The Natural Mirrors the Spiritual

In the natural, when a body dies, decomposition begins. The body stiffens. It releases toxins. It contaminates everything around it—soil, water, even the air. Spiritually, unforgiveness does the same:

It stiffens your spiritual flexibility. You can't move freely. Your gifts don't flow. Your joy dries up.

It poisons your atmosphere. Just like a decaying body releases bacteria, unforgiveness releases bitterness, anger, resentment, fear, and manipulation into your home, your relationships, and in how you parent.

It contaminates your legacy. Bitterness becomes generational trauma. It passes through families, leaving spiritual contamination for your children to inherit.

It blocks spiritual refreshment. Just like contaminated water is undrinkable, a heart full of unforgiveness cannot fully receive the Living Water. You stay spiritually dehydrated.

The Woman at the Well: A Picture of Dehydrated Souls

I think of the woman at the well (John 4). She had been rejected by five husbands. Rejection after rejection had left her desperate enough to risk her life for temporary comfort—living with a man who wasn't her husband just to fill the void. That's what unforgiveness does: it leaves us thirsty, chasing counterfeit comfort while blocking the true living water that only Christ can offer.

The Disease of Bitterness

Left unchecked, unforgiveness mutates into something even darker—witchcraft. Yes, witchcraft. Anytime we seek to emotionally manipulate others—whether through anger, silence, guilt-tripping, or revenge—we're crossing into dangerous spiritual territory. Romans 12:19 **(King James Version)** is clear:

"Vengeance is Mine; I will repay, saith the Lord."

We don't get to play God, no matter how justified we feel. I know this struggle intimately. In the middle of processing and healing one of the hardest traumas in my life, God instructed me to call the individual and tell them that He loves them. I obeyed, and the person responded with anger and more rejection. I hung up in tears and cried out to God,

"Lord, why would You set me up for more pain?"

And He answered,

"She is not rejecting you. She is rejecting Me."

That shifted my entire perspective. My prayers shifted from pain to empathy. Forgiveness unlocked a new level of healing, not just for me—but for my legacy.

Forgiveness Heals the Body, Too

Even the medical world acknowledges this truth. A Johns Hopkins study found that forgiveness lowers blood pressure, improves cholesterol, reduces anxiety, improves sleep, and even lowers the risk of heart attack. Your body literally thrives when you release unforgiveness. Nelson Schuman, author of *Freedom for Soul Wounds and Demons: Your Breakthrough to True Peace and Joy*, talks about forgiveness from the perspective of spiritual deliverance. What we don't understand about forgiveness is that they open gateways.

How Do You Reach Forgiveness?

Arriving to forgiveness must first start by acknowledging the pain. You don't dismiss it. You feel it. You mourn what was lost. And then you release it—not because they deserve it—but because *you* deserve freedom. Forgiveness doesn't mean the pain disappears overnight. Healing is a process. The scar may remain—but over time, even the scar fades until you barely see it. As long as you hold onto the rope, you're stuck on the cliff, sacrificing your healing to keep someone else alive. And that is not your assignment. I believe that God is calling you to let go of dead weight, for your healing, freedom, and legacy.

Step Six

THE BLUEPRINT FOR TRANSFORMATIONAL BOUNDARIES

I know the weight of living without boundaries. For years, I didn't have them—and it almost cost me my life, my voice, and my sense of worth. As a sexual abuse survivor—abused four different times at different points in my life—I knew the heavy silence of feeling powerless, unseen, and devalued. I carried that ache of believing no one respected me, cared for me, or even saw me. Healing has a way of rewriting your story. I often wear my "Healing" merch that I created, as a reminder that I no longer live as a victim but as a healed woman, walking in freedom, deliverance, and the boldness of knowing who I am in God. Boundaries became one of the tools that helped me reclaim my power and step into that new identity. Boundaries are more than just rules—they are the fences that protect your peace, your purpose, and your power.

What Are Boundaries?

When I teach children about boundaries, I describe them like a fence around a house. That fence represents your life. Inside of it, you have the right to place whatever matters to you—your values, your dreams, your energy, your voice. And if someone crosses that fence without permission, they are trespassing. Boundaries are parameters, the invisible lines that protect what's sacred. They communicate: *This is my safe space. You cannot enter without my consent.* Here's the truth: if you don't respect your own boundaries, you cannot expect others to respect them either.

Why Boundaries Matter

For a long time, I didn't understand who I was or what I carried. I lived by what people said about me. If someone called me smart, I believed I was smart. If they said I was beautiful, I believed I was beautiful. Their voices became my mirror. But when their voices turned toxic, I believed those lies too. Boundaries taught me that my voice is the loudest and most important in my life—second only to God's. What I speak to myself, what I choose to believe, and how I nurture my heart determine the direction of my life.

The Bible reminds us,

*"Out of the abundance of the heart, the mouth speaks."— Matthew 12:34 (**KJV**)*

What flows from your heart—your words, your choices, your self-talk—creates your reality. That is why boundaries are essential. They help you silence lies, guard your heart, and align your life with truth.

Boundaries in Action

One of the first lessons I learned was about financial boundaries. My personal rule is this: *I don't lend anything I can't afford to lose.* If I can't release it freely, I won't lend it, because otherwise I risk resentment, frustration, and broken trust. I also learned relational boundaries. If I tell someone not to call me after 10 p.m., that's a boundary. If they cross it, I won't hesitate to block them. Why?

Because boundaries don't work unless you enforce them. I no longer give in to emotional manipulation. Temper tantrums, guilt trips, and silent treatments—none of these move me anymore. My "no" means no. My "I can't" means I can't. Manipulation used to trap me, but healing showed me the freedom of standing firm.

The Boundaries Blueprint

1. **Know your worth.** Your identity doesn't come from others—it comes from God.
2. **Set clear parameters.** Define what is acceptable and what isn't in your life.
3. **Say no without guilt.** Refuse to give in to manipulation, gaslighting, or control.
4. **Enforce your limits.** Boundaries only work when they are honored and upheld.
5. **Guard your heart.** Protect your peace, your energy, and your purpose.

Boundaries are not about shutting people out—they are about keeping yourself whole. They are the guardrails that help you step boldly into the life God designed for you. Once you learn to honor your own boundaries, you'll find yourself walking lighter, freer, and more aligned with your divine assignment.

You are not what people say about you. You are who God says you are, and boundaries are the blueprint that will help you live like *it*.

The Power of Boundaries

Boundaries are one of those lessons I never get tired of teaching. Partially, because I had to learn how to implement them the hard way. I didn't grow up in an environment where boundaries were modeled. If you come from a family that isn't emotionally healthy, chances are, you weren't taught boundaries either—because people can't teach you what they don't know. Looking back, there were only two boundaries I remember my family repeating:

"Don't let anyone talk to you in any kind of way" and *"Don't have sex outside of marriage."*

Both were boundaries, but neither came with the practical tools to actually live them out. The truth is, boundaries require more than knowledge. They require practice, communication, and consistency. I wasn't taught how to say: *"I don't like that. That hurts me. Stop."* I had to learn those skills as an adult. The good news is that boundaries can be learned at any stage of life. When you master them, they become the guardrails that keep you from running off course.

Types of Boundaries

There are many types of boundaries—spiritual, emotional, financial, relational—but let's walk through a few that have transformed my life.

Time Boundaries

"Teach us to number our days, that we may apply our hearts unto wisdom."— *Psalm 90:12 **(KJV)***

That's a time boundary. It reminds us that life is short, and we must be intentional with how we spend it. Setting time boundaries means distinguishing between long-term goals and short-term assignments, then seeking God's wisdom on how to steward both.

Another example comes from *1 Chronicles 12:32*, which describes the sons of Issachar as men who understood the times and knew what Israel should do. Likewise, you must discern your own seasons. There are seasons for rest, for study, for transition, for growth. Missing the lessons of a season can cost you deeply.

I remember my early twenties when I had just given my life to Christ. I wasn't worried about dating or distractions. I was hungry for God. I would spend hours in His presence, studying scripture, learning how to hear His voice. That foundation has carried me through every other season since. Without it, I honestly don't know where I'd be.

Time boundaries also mean knowing when a season has ended. God will often prepare your heart for transition before it happens. I learned this firsthand when He instructed me to resign from a job without having another one lined up. It was terrifying—but necessary. The moment I obeyed; provision showed up in unexpected ways. Obedience created space for God's plan to unfold.

Personal Boundaries

"Above all else, guard your heart, for everything you do flows from it."—Proverbs 4:23 **(NIV)**

In Hebrew, the word "heart" is often interchangeable with "soul"—your mind, will, emotions, and experiences. This means that if your soul is carrying unhealed wounds, those wounds are driving the direction of your life. Many people are living lives God never intended, simply because they've never allowed Him to heal their souls. Boundaries are one way that He does that. They create the space for healing, clarity, and alignment with His purpose.

Financial Boundaries

"Owe no man anything except to love one another."—Romans 13:8 **(New King James Version)**

Financial boundaries have little to do with how much money you make, but rather how well you protect what you receive. In short, financial boundaries are about stewardship. Boundaries with money aren't about being stingy—they're about being wise. They keep you from becoming a personal bank for people who refuse to take responsibility for their own lives. Love does not mean enabling dysfunction. Financial boundaries protect both your resources and your relationships.

Emotional & Mental Boundaries

"Come to me, all you who are weary and burdened, and I will give you rest...for my yoke is easy, and my burden is light. "— Matthew 11:28-30 **(NIV)**

Your mental and emotional state are important to God. Being stressed out and burdened by the cares of life was never his idea. In fact, he knew we would face life struggles and provided a remedy.

Your first emotional boundary is learning to go to God with your weariness. Journal. Pray. Sit in His presence. Exchange your burdens for His promises. That's how you protect your mental health and avoid carrying weights that were never yours to carry. Another avenue that has been given for establishing emotional and mental boundaries is by hiring a mental health professional to help you get the tools you need in order to cope with life.

Sexual Boundaries

70 | P a g e

"…your body is a temple of the Holy Spirit…"— *1 Corinthians 6:19-20* **(KJV)**

That truth applies whether single or married. Marriage does not erase the need for boundaries—it simply shifts them. One of the most heartbreaking conversations I've had was with a married woman who felt violated by her husband because he ignored her "no." I told her plainly: Marriage does not make violation acceptable. A covenant built on love requires sacrifice, honor, and mutual respect. Boundaries protect intimacy, not hinder it.

Why Boundaries Matter

They protect emotional well-being. Without them, burnout, resentment, and exhaustion are inevitable.

They increase productivity and focus. Boundaries eliminate distractions and keep you aligned with your goals.

They prevent people-pleasing. Saying "no" frees you to say "yes" to what truly matters.

They set the standard for respect. You teach people how to treat you by what you tolerate.

They strengthen leadership presence. Strong boundaries build confidence, clarity, and trust.

They create balance. Boundaries help you prioritize between work, ministry, family, and self-care.

They encourage healthy relationships. Boundaries foster mutual respect, not resentment.

They reduce decision fatigue. When you know your values, decisions become simple.

They boost self-respect and confidence. Every time you enforce a boundary, you affirm your worth.

Boundaries Are Love

At their core, boundaries are not walls—they are gates. They don't keep love out; they keep chaos out so that love can flourish. When you honor your time, your heart, your money, and your body, you are saying:

I am valuable. I am worthy. I am stewarding what God entrusted to me.

When others encounter you, they will either rise to the standard you set—or remove themselves. Either way, your peace remains protected. Boundaries are not selfish. They are the stewardship of your heart and purpose. They imply that you are using wisdom over some of the greatest assets of your life. They are an act of love—to God, to yourself, and to others.

Take a few minutes to sit with these questions. Don't rush. Allow yourself to write freely, without judgment. This is your safe space to reflect, release, and realign.

1. Where in my life have I struggled to set or honor boundaries, and how has that shaped the way I see myself?
2. What emotions rise up in me when I think about saying "no"? Do I feel guilt, shame, fear of rejection — or something else?

3. Who in my life has been the most resistant to my boundaries? What does that resistance reveal about their role in my healing journey?

4. When was a time I felt completely drained by someone's demands or presence? What would have been different if I had set a clear boundary?

5. What is one boundary I know I need to establish right now — and what's holding me back from doing it?

6. When I imagine a healed version of myself walking in her full power, what boundaries does she have in place? How does she carry herself differently?

7. How might my relationships, career, or emotional health transform if I began to see boundaries not as walls, but as bridges to peace and freedom?

TRANSFORMATION LEADERSHIP

While in graduate school, I had a dream that has remained with me. It came during a season that I was wrestling with old wounds and unprocessed trauma. In the dream, I found myself in a vast body of water—dark, deep, and intimidating. All around me were firefighters and police officers—people who should have known how to swim—yet were all drowning.

Suddenly, I heard a still small voice say to me: *"Tiffany, stand up."*

So, I did. And when I stood, I realized the water barely reached my knees. We weren't drowning at all. We only thought we were. I began telling everyone else,

"Just stand up! It's not as deep as it seems."

When I shared the dream with my professor, he said something I'd never considered:

"Tiffany, this sounds like leadership. You saw what others couldn't, and you had the courage to act first."

Until that moment, I had never thought of myself as a leader. Looking back, I could see the pattern. Time and time again, I was placed in positions where people looked to me for direction, strength, and answers. This dream was a start of me learning to embrace a truth that many of us overlook: leadership isn't always about standing at the front of the room, it is about influence. It's about having the courage to stand when others feel like they're drowning. When you dare to stand, you give others permission to do the same.

What Is Transformational Leadership?

There are many kinds of leadership, but transformational leadership is different. Traditional leadership provides structure, oversight, and direction. Transformational leadership goes further—it inspires change from the inside out. A transformational leader doesn't just manage tasks; they cultivate people. They don't simply point to the destination; they walk alongside others, helping them grow stronger through the journey. Transformational leaders *create other leaders.* Think of it this way: a manager may give you instructions, but a transformational leader ignites something within you that makes you want to rise higher. They see strengths in you that you may not yet see in yourself. This is the kind of leadership that leaves a legacy.

The Foundation: Authenticity

The heartbeat of transformational leadership is authenticity. You cannot transform lives if you are not first rooted in who you are. Too many of us have spent years apologizing for existing—shrinking back, playing small, or moving aside as though someone else's life mattered more than ours. For years, I would literally step out of the way in grocery store aisles, apologizing when I had done nothing wrong, avoiding eye contact because I felt unworthy of being seen.

Healing taught me a powerful truth: apologizing for your existence is an insult to God. He created you intentionally—your personality, your gifts, even your quirks. Yes, there are parts of us that need refining, but the core of who you are is not a mistake. Transformational leaders stop shrinking. They stop apologizing. They show up fully, unapologetically, and authentically, because they understand their presence is an assignment.

The Skills of a Transformational Leader

If we want to rise as transformational leaders—especially as women in this generation—we must intentionally cultivate the following skills:

Cultivate Self-Confidence

Leadership requires confidence, not arrogance. Confidence is simply the belief that God has equipped you with what you need to step into your assignment. Self-confidence looks like making decisions without second-guessing yourself into paralysis. It also looks like loving yourself enough to embrace your uniqueness instead of seeing it as a weakness. It looks like giving yourself grace when you fall short, knowing you are still in process. Cultivating confidence means practicing small, intentional acts of self-love—like dining alone at a restaurant, without distraction, and learning to enjoy your own company. It means learning to maintain eye contact instead of shying away. These practices aren't just about confidence; they are training for leadership. Here's the truth, you cannot be a transformational leader if you're bound by fearing people.

Master Assertive Communication

Assertiveness for women is often mislabeled as aggression. Assertive communication isn't about being harsh; it's about being clear, firm, and confident without apology. I'm reminded of a time when I purchased some Redfish from a local grocery store. I got home and discovered that it was spoiled. When I returned it, the manager questioned me and implied that I was lying about the time I purchased the fish, despite the time stamp on the receipt. He gaslit me at every turn, insisting the receipt didn't match, the tag wasn't there, the fish must have sat in my car too long.

In that moment, I could have backed down, over-explained, or apologized. Instead, I calmly looked him in the eye and said,

"Sir, I have no reason to lie. Everything you need is on the receipt. The tag is on the fish. I'm simply asking for an exchange."

That is assertive communication: speaking the truth with clarity and confidence, without shrinking and without aggression.

Practical Tools for Assertive Communication

Use "I" Statements

Using "I" statements will help you own your perspective without blaming. When implementing practice using the phrase "I feel _____" and insert a feeling. Naming your feeling helps in two ways: with identifying your feelings and with learning how to self-validate.

Maintain Eye Contact

A good communicator, maintains eye contact, even when it feels uncomfortable. Different cultures have different rules about eye contact so ensure that you have done your homework in advance. In my country, maintaining eye contact conveys trust, authority, and confidence.

Listen to Understand

Active listening involves you listening for understanding rather than listening to respond. It communicates that you are patient and have respect for the other person(s) involved in the conversation.

Practice Accountability

Conflict is inevitable. Resist giving into your emotions by owning your mistakes. You can help others be accountable by stating the facts about a situation. Keep good notes on your accomplishments, wins, and experiences in case you will have to recall them.

Offer Solutions

Leaders are natural solutionists. You have the ability to create something out of nothing. Therefore, anytime you have a complaint or an observation, seek God for possible solutions before presenting them aloud. Problem solvers always experience promotion.

Be Firm

Share your thoughts and experiences firmly and in a matter-of-fact fashion. This is not aggression. Insecure responses will try to gaslight and call you aggressive, passionate, or label you an alpha woman. Remain calm, state facts, and don't back down. Remember the example I shared about the store manager?

Develop Emotional Intelligence

Emotional intelligence (EQ) is the ability to recognize, understand, and manage both your own emotions and the emotions of others. Great leaders are not those who never feel anger, fear, or disappointment—they are those who know how to regulate those emotions and lead with wisdom even in conflict. Emotional intelligence looks like:

- Recognizing when you're triggered and pausing instead of exploding.
- Refusing to be pulled into someone else's chaos.
- Apologizing when you're wrong and repairing relationships with humility.
- Listening deeply so others feel heard and valued.
- Affirming others when needed.

Emotional intelligence helps us live that out—choosing to resolve, release, and repair rather than carry bitterness into tomorrow.

Why Women, Why Now?

I believe with all my heart that God is positioning women for such a time as this. We are seeing doors open and assignments unfold that generations before us could only dream about. This isn't by accident—it is divine recompense for years of inequality, silencing, and being overlooked. With this positioning comes responsibility. We cannot step into these places while shrinking back. We cannot apologize for our presence or downplay our gifts. Transformational leadership calls us to stand tall, authentic, and unapologetic, knowing that our assignment is not about us—it's about those we are called to impact.

When you refuse to apologize for existing and lead with confidence, clarity, and compassion, you become more than a leader. You become a catalyst for transformation. Remember that dream from grad school? The water wasn't as deep as it looked. That's true for leadership, too. Sometimes the situations around us feel so overwhelming that it looks like we might drown. But transformational leaders hear the whisper:

"Stand up…"

and don't back down from the challenge. As we stand, we discover that what once threatened to consume us is only knee-deep. Then, with courage and clarity, we turn to others and say, *"Stand up. You don't have to drown when you were born to lead."*

THE COMMISSION TO HEAL FORWARD

One of the greatest enemies to unlocking the Real You is the quiet belief that you have more time. More time to heal, obey, or become the person you always dreamed of becoming. We tell ourselves that who God created us to be can wait until life slows down. Until the kids are older. Until we feel more confident. Until we're less afraid. The truth is this: The person you are called to be does not live in later. She lives in now. Jesus confronted this mindset directly in John 4:35 (**NIV**):

"Don't you have a saying, 'It's still four months more and then the harvest? I tell you, open your eyes and look at the fields! They are ripe for harvest."

In other words, Stop postponing obedience because the harvest isn't coming. It's here. What's missing isn't opportunity. It's participation and you are the laborer. I used to believe I had more time.

More time to use my voice.
More time to overcome fear.
More time to become bold.

Then one day I looked up — and realized time had moved while I was still negotiating with hesitation.

First, we think we're too young. Then we're too busy. Then suddenly, we're too tired. Too responsible. Too late. Obedience does not wait for perfect conditions. If you've read this far, confronted mother wounds, faced father wounds, dismantled doubt, and rebuilt identity — then you already know: You are not waiting on God. God is waiting on you.

The Silent Assassins of Destiny

You've learned throughout this book that identity is the foundation, but identity must be defended. The enemy does not attack randomly — he attacks strategically.

He whispers:

You have more time.

You're not ready.

You're not qualified.

What if you fail?

Who do you think you are?

Self-doubt is quiet. It doesn't scream. It suggests, and if you agree with it long enough, it reshapes your reality. Many of those whispers didn't start in adulthood. They began in childhood — through rejection, abandonment, inconsistency, or trauma. Those early wounds formed internal narratives:

I'm not enough.

Love leaves.

I must earn approval.

My voice doesn't matter.

Left unchallenged, those narratives mature with you. Self-doubt will make you question what God already confirmed. It will keep you in rooms that are beneath your true capacity and will align you with people that reinforce your limitations. If self-doubt remains, your confidence will erode. Where there is chronic self-doubt, there will be fragile confidence, but confidence is not arrogance. It is anchored faith.

"And this is the confidence we have…" **— 1 John 5:14 (KJV)**

God-Confidence is not arrogant yet loud. It says:

I may feel unqualified, but I am called.

I may feel afraid, but I am equipped.

I may feel small, but I serve a big God.

Authentic confidence is not rooted in performance; it is rooted in identity. Real identity is what this entire journey has been about.

Unhealthy Relationships

Unhealthy relationships will drain clarity. Toxic environments suffocate vision. Emotional chaos distracts from calling. When you are exhausted, stagnation feels normal. You survive instead of building. You cope instead of creating. Stagnation is not your inheritance. The Real You is not stagnant. She is decisive, aware, and sets healthy boundaries. She heals instead of hides.

Fear

Fear has been a personal battleground that for me since childhood. I fell in love with music at five years old. It was so bad that I would hold imaginary church services in our living room while playing the piano and singing with everything in me. Every time

I would play the piano, I would feel God's presence, but singing in front of people? That terrified me. Fear told me my voice wasn't enough.

By my adult years, that fear had matured into full anxiety. During my undergraduate college career, I would overthink presentations for days. Each time that I would stand up to speak, my mind would go blank. Fear didn't just touch my voice. It touched my relationships and opportunities, and was robbing me of my calling. It has a way of exaggerating its power until you confront it. Fear is loud — but it is not sovereign. The real you cannot emerge if fear is being allowed to lead.

You have spent this book uncovering, unlearning, rebuilding, and reclaiming. You are not who you were when you started these pages. The wounds may have shaped you, but they do not get the final word. The lies may have followed you, but they no longer lead you. The real you is not fragile. She is empowered. She is not confused. She is clear. She is not waiting. She is ready. So, walk boldly. Speak decisively. Build courageously. Love wisely. Set boundaries unapologetically. And when fear whispers, answer it with movement. You were never created to live hidden, hesitant, or half-healed.

Steps to Healing Forward

Declare

Write one Scripture that confronts your loudest lie. Speak it daily for the next seven days.

Decide

Choose one action you have delayed — and complete it within seven days. Not plan. Complete.

Detach

Identify one draining pattern. Establish one boundary to protect your peace.

Daily Question

Each morning, ask yourself:

Am I living as the Real Me today — or the wounded version?

You were created to occupy space and to be the light wherever you go. This is your Real ID. Not potential. Not someday. Now!

Healing Resources

My Declaration of Independence in God

For I am persuaded that neither death, nor life, nor angels, nor principalities, nor powers, nor things present, nor things to come, 39. Nor height, nor depth, nor any other creature shall be able to separate me from the love of God, which is in Christ Jesus our Lord.

*Romans 8: 38-39 (**KJV**)*

Declarations

Thoughts, Actions and Emotions
I refuse to let my emotions control my actions.
Proverbs 3: 25-26

I refuse to let what comes out of my mouth control me.
Matthew 15:18

Abandonment God wants me.
Acts 17:37-38

People-Pleasing
People do not define who I am. My standards for who I am are set by God.
Psalms 139:14

Condemnations/struggling with personal issues
My past does not define my present and/or future outcomes.
Jeremiah 29:11

I will not allow my circumstances to cripple me. Things will not always be like this.
Philippians 4: 11,13

I will not limit myself or limit what God can do through me.
Luke 18:27

Legacy
I will leave behind a good legacy for my children.
1 Peter 2:9

I will guide my children down a good path.
Acts 16:15

When I become stronger, I will sow into others. When strengthen, strengthen someone else.

Mathew 27: 40

Purpose
I will be who God called me to be.
Jeremiah 1: 5

Finances
Secure the Bag by Securing my relationship with Christ.
Matthew 6:33

I am a giver.
Acts 20: 35

Reassurance
God got me.
Romans 8:28

NEW STRENGTH
In my weakest moments, God will be my strength
2 Corinthians 12: 9

Struggling with Fear
Fear will not get in the way of doing a mighty work for God.
2 Timothy 1:7

I will not let satan take my joy, family, friends, relationship, future, children, ministry and the words that God has given and is going to give me and my desire to seek God.
Psalms 139: 18-19

Scriptures on Abandonment

____

____

____

Scriptures on Rejections

____

____

____

Scriptures on self-esteem/self-love

____

____

____

Scriptures on emotional healing

____

____

____

STEAL MY HEALING STRATEGY

1. Taught me how to set boundaries (moved away from bad influences).

2. Began creating a life I wanted (gave myself permission to live life on my terms and not others).

3. Gained likeminded friends that held me accountable and where supportive (friends that would challenge me and support and encourage me).

4. Spent time learning to love myself, God and my children.

5. Began dealing with emotional issues (wrote out issues, therapy, searching scriptures. Learning the word).

6. Repeated confessions over my life and kept a
    journal of when God answered my prayers
    and confessions

Note From the Author

If you met me in real life, one of the first things you would notice is this—I don't just talk about healing… I live it.

My work was not only built from theory. It was built from also doing the hard, honest, often uncomfortable work of confronting my own emotional wounds, breaking unhealthy patterns, and choosing wholeness—again and again.

And now, I help other women do the same.

I am an emotional healing coach and the voice behind a growing movement of women who are ready to stop performing strength and actually become whole. I work with high-capacity women who have learned how to show up for everyone else—but somewhere along the way, lost connection with themselves.

The women I serve are not weak. They are capable, driven, and resilient.

But they are also tired.
Tired of repeating cycles.
Tired of feeling stuck in places they've outgrown.
Tired of knowing there's more in them—but not fully accessing it.

That's where my work begins.

Through coaching, teaching, and transformational spaces like *Healed University*, I've created an environment where women can finally be honest about what's really going on beneath the surface—and get the tools, language, and support to heal it at the root.

Because surface-level change was never the goal.

Wholeness is.

If you've made it to this point in the book, then you already know—this wasn't just a casual read.

Something in these pages spoke directly to you.

Maybe it stretched you.
Maybe it exposed something.

Maybe it made you realize you can't keep showing up the same way anymore.

And if that's the case, I want to challenge you…

Don't close this book and go back to life as usual.

You don't need more time. You need a next step.

Join Healed University

Healed University was created for this exact moment—the moment where you realize healing is no longer optional if you want to become who you know you're called to be.

Join the waitlist to be the first to know when doors open and connect with us for powerful tools to help you begin your healing journey now.

www.drtiffanyross.com/healedu

The version of you you've been searching for is on the other side of your healing.

Don't delay meeting her.

References

Introduction

Goldenberg, Herbert. *Family Therapy: An Overview*. 7th ed. Belmont, CA: Thomson Brooks/Cole, 2008.

Smith, Joshua P. "Post Ministry Recovery." Online workshop, May 9, 2023.

World Health Organization. "COVID-19 Pandemic Triggers 25% Increase in Prevalence of Anxiety and Depression Worldwide." March 2, 2022. https://www.who.int/news/item/02-03-2022-covid-19-pandemic-triggers-25-increase-in-prevalence-of-anxiety-and-depression-worldwide